Retail Marketing:
A study of Consumer Behavior with special Reference to selected Malls in Ahmedabad

:: Author ::

Dr. Chirag Raval

(M.Com., M.Phil., Ph.D.)

PUBLISHED BY

Hemchandracharya International Publishing House
HQ. At & Po. Chaveli., Ta- Chansma,
Dist- Patan, North Gujarat, India, Asia.
www.iphouseindia.com

First Publication: 12th February, 2015

ISBN:- 978-15-08712-25-1

Price: Rs.750/- INDIA

$ 15 OUTSIDE INDIA

PUBLISHED BY

**Hemchandracharya International Publishing House
HQ. At & Po. Chaveli., Ta- Chansma,
Dist- Patan, North Gujarat, India, Asia.
www.iphouseindia.com**

Contents

Chapter Scheme

Chapter-1

Introduction

INTRODUCTION

Today human needs have become more sophisticated and complex in nature and at the same time there are umpteen numbers of firms who see great opportunity for business potential and the intensity of battle for space has become very significant. This has given rise to marketing activities which are essentially marketing plans and programs with a view to countering competition and at the same time retain the business. The marketing activity has been in the business for long but it was not recognized as an organized function and an organized activity very crucial to the growth of an organization.

The Marketing plays a pivotal role in the growth and development of a country irrespective of a country irrespective of size, population and the concepts are so interlinked that, in the absence of one, another virtually cannot survive. It is a historical fact that the development of marketing has always kept pace with the economic growth of the country. Both have experienced evolutionary rather than revolutionary change. The objective of modern marketing is to make profits through satisfying consumer's needs and wants. Hence, the marketers have to understand the real needs, wants, beliefs and attitudes of the consumers towards their products and services. Today network marketing is a multibillion dollar business. Numbers of companies have adopted this business model. It has grown into one of the driving forces of the 21st century economy.

CONSUMER BEHAVIOR

All of us are consumers. We consume things of daily use, we also consume and buy these products according to our needs, preferences and buying power. These can be consumable goods, durable goods, specialty goods or, industrial goods.

What we buy, how we buy, where and when we buy, in how much quantity we buy depends on our perception, self concept, social and cultural background and our age and family cycle, our attitudes, beliefs values, motivation, personality, social class and many other factors that are both internal and external to us. While buying, we also consider whether to buy or not to buy and from which source or seller to buy. In some societies there is a lot of affluence and, these societies can afford to buy in greater quantities and at shorter intervals. In poor societies, the consumer can rarely meet his barest needs.

The marketers therefore try to understand the needs of different consumers and having understood his different behaviors which require an in depth study of their internal and external environment, they formulate their plans for marketing.

Management is a youngest of sciences and oldest of arts and consumer behavior in management is a very young discipline. Various scholars and academicians concentrated on it at a much later stage. It was during the 1950s that marketing concept developed, and thus the need to study the behavior of consumers was recognized. Marketing starts with the needs of the customer and ends with his satisfaction. When everything revolves round the customer, then the study of consumer behavior becomes a necessity. It starts with the buying of goods. Goods can be bought individually, or in groups.

Definition of consumer behavior

Consumer behavior can be defined as the decision making process and physical activity involved in acquiring, evaluating, using and disposing of goods and services.

This definition clearly brings out that it is not just the buying of goods / services that receives attention in consumer behavior but, the process starts much before the goods have been acquired or bought. A process of buying starts in the minds of the consumer, which leads to the finding of alternatives between products that can be acquired with their relative advantages and disadvantages. This leads to internal and external research. Then follows a process of decision making for purchase and using the goods, and then the post purchase behavior which is also very important because it gives a clue to the marketers whether his product has been a success or not.

To understand the likes and dislikes of the consumer, extensive consumer research studies are being conducted. These researchers try to find out.

- What the consumer thinks of the company's products and those of its competitors?
- How can the product be improved in their opinion?
- How the customers use the product?
- What is the customer's attitude towards the product and its advertising?
- What is the role of customer in his family?

Importance of consumer behavior

This subject is useful to the marketers, consumer behavior; we learn the logic behind consumption related behavior. It makes us wiser consumers. Marketers benefit by understanding how consumers take consumption decisions which enable them to formulate suitable marketing strategies. They can anticipate the reactions of the consumers to various cues, both informational and organizational. It is likely to give them a competitive advantage.

As students of consumer behavior, we learn the logic behind consumption related decisions and motivations which propel them to take certain decisions. It becomes a fascinating subject, drawing from various disciplines like psychology sociology, social psychology, anthropology and economics. To begin with a consumer was conceived as economic man taking rational decisions. Later theories brought an end to this economic man.

Growth of consumer behavior

Consumer behavior is a multi disciplinary field which draws its concept from several fields of study. It is useful to the marketing organizations, consumer groups and governmental authorities. It is an applied field since the concepts of behavioral science disciplines are applied to the understanding of human behavior as far as consumption is concerned. By its very nature, it increases appreciative content of marketing, and leads to more effective and consumer oriented marketing programs. Consumer behavior is interwoven with the emergence of the marketing discipline and has extended the motivation research of 1950s. By 60s consumer behavior acquired a formidable body of knowledge.

Chapter-2

REVIEW OF LITERATURE

1. Meyer tries to bring out the importance of first impressions in selecting retail outlet by a customer. He discusses as to how first impression are formed and how a successful retailer can use this knowledge to his or her advantage.

   (Meyer, G.Warren, Harris, G.Edward., Kohns, P.Donald., and stone III, R.James. Retail Marketing, 8th edition, Mc-graw Hill international, Singapore – 1988.)

2. In one of the chapters entitled "the retailing revolution", Davison, et.al., highlights the origin and the decades of changes that has taken place in global retailing since the end of world war II and thereafter. He says that change is now a constant factor in retailing. Almost any social, economic or political event of consequence will affect how consumers decide and behave in the market place. Retailers must recognize charge, adapt to it, and prosper from it if not, their competitors most surely

will.

(Davidson, R. William., Sweeney J. Daniel, and Stampfl, W.Ronald, Retailing Management, John Wiley & Sons, USA, 1988.)

3. Walters investigates the impact of retail price promotions on consumer purchasing patterns and the performance of competing retailers. (Walters G. Rockney, "Assessing the impact of retail price, promotions on product substitution, complementary purchase and interstore sales displacement", Journal of Marketing, Vol. 55, No.2, April 1991, p.17-29.)

4. Devasahayam gives us the main reasons why customers norMally do not shift loyalties from the sMall retailer to supermarkets in this study. (Devasahayam, Madona "A big Dea", Praxis – Business Line's Journal on Management, Vol. 2, No. 2, August 1998.)

5. To document the changes in retail environment from its early days, the ETTG report volume I had conducted a comprehensive study of the Indian

retailing environment. It brings out the current business status and its potential in India, as well as the practices and management philosophy on all key facts of retail business, like the retail consumers, different retail formats, retail location, and customer management and so on.

(Economic times intelligence group report, Retail, 1st edition, Economic times, 2000, 11.)

6. Today shoppers want the total customer experience: superior solutions to their needs, respect, an emotional connection, fair price and convenience. Berry in his article brings out five pillars for the success of any retail business. (Bery, B.Leonard, "The old pillars of new retailing" Harvard business Review, April 2001, p.131-137.)

7. While customers should feel they are getting the most efficient service, employees on the other hand need to be highly motivated and have a fulfilled experience at work. Wold[5] in her article gives ten tactics to boost morale of the employees working in the retail outlet.

(Wold, Barbara "Retail your customers and staff" Images retail, Vol. No. 2, January 2003, p.42.)

8. Kaushesh analysis the trends of past and present retailing and illustrates how the past can provide a road map for the present retailers. It explains several strategies used by different retailers – ranging from the traditional strategy based on low price and convenience to the recent strategies based on value, customer relationship and customer experience. It also helps in identifying the most suitable mix of strategies for present retailers.

(Kaushesh, Anshul. "Retailing: The way forward" Marketing mastermind, April 2004, p.41-46.)

9. The report prepared by business world provides insights on an overview of India, consumer psychographics, about retail in India and Asia and also retail and consumer trends in Asia and India in specific.

(The marketing white book: the essential hand book for Marketers, Business World, 2nd Edition, 2005.)

10. Barbara finds customers top ten sales and customer service requirements in her study.

(Wold, Barbara "Retain your customers and staff" images retail, vol. 16 – July 15, 2005, p.26-27.)

11. Lusch, et.al., in one of the chapters "understanding the retail customers", discuses about the retail patronage model. It is a process model, moving from left to right. The process begins when the consumer recognizes a need to shop. The consumer then evaluates shopping alternatives and selects a store or stores to visit. Each store as it is visited is continuously evaluated so the consumer can decide whether study in the store and shop or leave. The consumer will reach closure if offerings in the store are favorably evaluated. Finally we move to the outcomes stage, in which the consumer purchases, postpones purchases, and does additional searching, or decides not to buy. Consumer is continuously storing information for future use in shopping situations and therefore, the model has a feedback loop. In addition each stage of the model

is affected by the information sources that continually bombarded the consumer.

(Lysch, F. Robert, Dunne Patrick, and Gable, Myron, Op. Cit.)

12. Venkateshwarlu H finds organized retailing globally, Retail industry – GDP and employment and FDI in Indian retailing opportunities and threats in his study.

(Venkateshwaralu H. and Ranjani c.v. "FDI in retailing A boon or a bane?" The Indian Journal of commerce, Vol. 60, No.1, January – March - 2007, p.1-9.)

13. Dey tries to bring out growth of retailing and limitation and challenges in retailing in the study. (Dey Dipankar, "GAIs and Transnational Retailing – few concerns and challenges". The ICFAI Journal of Management Research, Vol. 6, No. 6, 2007, p.63-76.)

14. Anbalagan tries to bring out the growth of retail consumer market, opportunities, emerging trends in retail consumer marketing and reason for the

change in the Indian consumer in the study.

(Anbalagan M.A. Gunasekaram V., "Retail Consumers market in India – the next big leap" Indian Journal of Marketing, Vol. 37, No.3, March – 2007, p.24-29.)

15. Devdeep gives us the idea focus on Mall bubble and what's the lack of Indian Mall in his study.

(Singh Devdeep, Soni Aditi "The Mall bubble" 4Ps – Business and Marketing, Vol. II, Issue. 11, 6th July – 19th July 2007, p.95-99.)

16. Srivastava investigates retail situation in India as well as global perspective and international entries in Indian retail and also gives suggestions to retailers and government for improvement in her study.

(Srivastava Ruchi and Srivastava Binkey. "Retail its global perspective" synergy. Journal of I.T. & Management, Vols. No. 2, July 2007, p.108-115.)

17. Gupta Anupama investigates retailing human resources challenges ahead and FDI in retail sectors in her study.

(Gupta Anupama, "Retailing Human Resource Challenges Ahead" Synergy – 1.7 S Journal of I.T. & Management, Vol. 5, No.2, July 2007, p.12-107.)

18. The article published in Indian Journal of Marketing provides insights on impact of Mall on retail trade, the reasons for retail Boom in twin cities, reasons for slow adoption of Malls.

(Venkateshwarlu H., Rajani C.V., "SMall Vs Mall" – Indian Journal of Marketing, Vol. 37, No.10, October 2007, p.29-33.)

19. Baseer gives us the prospects and problems of Indian retailing trends in Indian retailing industry and the biggest problem of retail outlets in his study.

(Baseer Amatal, Laxmi Prabta G. "Prospects and problems of Indian Retailing" – Indian journal of Marketing, Vol. 37, No. 10, October, 2007, p.26-28.)

20. Malliswari investigates the emerging trends and strategies in Indian retailing and growth of hypermarkets and Malls in the study.

(Malliswari M.N. "Emerging trends and strategies

in Indian Retailing Indian Journal of Marketing vol. 37, No. 11, November – 2007, p.21-27.)

CHAPTER 3
RESEARCH DESIGN

Rational of the study

A study was proposed to explore and recreated an opinion of consumer behavior towards selected Malls at Ahmedabad.

Objectives of the study:

1. To identify the factors influencing the consumer behavior while selecting a particular Mall.

2. To extract the source of information through which, consumer came to know about various Malls

3. To identify problems faced by consumer while purchasing through Mall.

4. To know the facilities provided to the consumers by the Mall organization

Hypothesis

Ho: There is no significance relation between the facilities provided by the Mall and customer satisfaction.

H₁: There is significance relation between the facilities provided by the Mall and customer satisfaction.

Research Design: Descriptive type of research

The study is based on descriptive type of research, which is very regal design of study and procedure to be used, must be carefully planned. The study is bifurcating into various stages such as objectives, methods of data collection and selection of sample size.

Sources of data

In order to achieve the objectives of the present study, there are two types of data collection methods

(a) Primary data

(b) Secondary data

(a) Primary Data

Primary data were collected directly by the researcher for the first time to the best of the knowledge and belief of the researcher, asset of interviewers with consumers.

Questionnaire

A separate questionnaire was prepared for consumer to obtain the necessary feedback and data. Consumers were interviewed and requested to answer the questionnaire. They were contacted personally to avoid misunderstanding, misinterpretation and possible confusion.

(b) **Secondary Data**

The research would like to utilize the available books, magazines, Newspapers, Websites and other published source to provide relevant information and current information about the Malls, and consumer behavior.

Data collection method

In this study, I used a personal survey method which is the face to face questioning and answering to consumers.

Field work

The present study was carried out at selected Malls in Ahmedabad, Gujarat.

Sampling plan

Sample Unit

The sample unit in appropriate size would be drawn from various respondents

Sample size

A sample of hundred (100) consumers and four (4) Malls from Ahmedabad city.

Sampling method

Non-probability quota sampling method was used

Significance of the study

Retailing demands a thorough understanding of local customs, consumer's tastes and culture. Malls provide refined services to customers, often treated as respected guests. The customers or consumers are always right; the consumer is king this principle is implemented in the business.

In retailing the formulation of product mix and other 3Ps that is price, place, and promotion mix became significant as new, sophisticated and refined service bear.

The efficiency of wooing customers. Beside this, sound behavioral management helps in excelling competition and also to know the desired result or to make the managerial decisions proactive, it is essential to assign due weight age to the behavioral management.

This study helps to retailers towards the consumer's behavior and than they implement in their retail Organization.

Limitations of the study

As every coin has two sides, the research study also has two sides there are certain limitations, which deceives the object of the study.

1. **Area**

    The research study has been conducted only at selected Malls in Ahmedabad.

2. **Time**

    The research was done in very limited time of 6 to 7 months.

3. **Sample size**

    The sample size prefixed for the research study was of Hundred (100) consumers and four (4) Malls which are limited.

Chapter-4

Management of Retail Marketing

The word retail is derived from the French word 'retailer', meaning to cut a piece of or to break bulk. In simple terms, it implies a firsthand transaction with the customer.

The word 'Retail' is derived from a French ford with the prefix 're' and the verb 'trailer' meaning "to cut again". Thus, retail trade is one that cuts off sMaller portions from large lumps of goods. It is a process through which goods are transported to final consumers. It consists of the all activities involved in selling, renting and providing goods and services to ultimate customers for personal, family and household use.

Retailing is an important marketing activity. Not only do producers and consumers meet through retailing actions, but retailing also creates customer value & has a significant impact on the economy.

To consumer, the value of retailing is in the form of utilities provided. Retailing's economic value is represented by the people employed in retailing as well as by the total amount of money exchanged in retail sales,

Meaning of Retail, Retailer and Retailing

Some definition can be given to clearly explain the meaning of retail retailer & retailing.

1. Retail

"Sale of goods to the public in sMall quantities." - Oxford Dictionary.

2. Retailer

Business whose sales come primarily from retailing. - Philip Kotler & Armstrong.

3. Retailing

Retailing includes all activities incident to selling to the ultimate consumers. - American Definition Committee.

4. Retailing

Retailing is selling final consumer products to householders. - Mc Cartly.

5. Retailing

"All Activities involved in selling goods or services directly to final consumer for their personal, non-business use." - Philip Kotler & Armstrong.

6. Retail

David Gilbert has defined retail as any business that directs it marketing efforts towards satisfying the final consumer based upon the organization of selling goods and services as a means of distribution.

7. Retailing

Retailing can be referred to all the activities involved in the marketing and distribution of goods and services.

Retailing and the marketing mix

Retaining forms integral parts of the marketing mix and include elements like product, place, price, people, presentation and promotion. Place relates to the distribution and availability of products in various locations.

Customers are first introduced and services through these retailer outlets and get feedback on the performance of their products and customers expectations about them.

Retail stores serve the communication hubs for customers. Commonly known as the point of sale or the Point of Purchase (POP), retail stores transmit information to the customers through advertisements and display. Hence, the role of retailing in the marketing mix is very significant.

Retailing Scenario-Indian

The retail scenario in India is unique. Much of it is in the unorganized sector, with over 12 million retail outlets of various sizes and formats. Almost 96% of these retail outlets are less than 500 sq.ft. in size the per capita retail space in India being 2 sq.ft. compared to the US figure of 16 sq. ft. India's per capita retailing space is thus the lowest in the world.

With more than 9 outlets per 10000 people, India has the largest number in the world. Most of them are independent and contribute as much as 96% to total retail sales.

Because of the increasing number of nuclear families, working women, greater work pressure and increased commuting time, convenience has become a priority for India consumers. They want everything under one roof for easy access and multiplicity of choice. This offers an excellent opportunity for organized retailers in the country who account for just 2% of the estimated US$ 180 billion worth of goods that are retailed in India every year. This figure is equivalent to the turnover of one single US based retail chain, WalMart.

The growth and development of organized retailing in India is driven by two main factors lower prices and benefits the consumers can't resist. According to experts, economics of scale drive down the cost of the supply chain, allowing retailers to offer more benefits offered to the customer.

According to the Global Retail development index of 2005 conducted by AT Kearney India was ranked 1 among 30 most attractive retailing destinations across the globe.

- Unorganized sector comprise of grocery stores, drug stores, cosmetics, readymade garments, white goods, agri inputs etc.

Organized retailing in different product categories

- Apparel retailing (Westside, Pantaloon Raymond)
- Food retailing (food world of RPG Group and Food Bazaar of Pantaloon).
- Health and beauty products (planet health)
- Foot wear (Nike, Bata, Liberty)
- Music and entertainment (Music world of TOI)
- Book retailing (Crosswords, Landmark and Oxford)
- Watches and Jewelry (Tanishq. Titan)
- Fuel retailing (Indian Oil, Reliance, IBP, BPCL).
- Home furniture (Durian, Gautier, Perin)
- Luggage (VIP, Samsonite)

Reasons for growth of retailing in India

- The rapidly growing middle class consumers
- Increase in per capita spending by consumers
- Growth in the number of double income households
- Less time at the disposal of DI families

- Exposure to world class tastes and preferences of products and brands through advertising.

- Rising workforce with global travel

- Increasing usage of credit / debit cards

- Growing youth population with ability to study and work simultaneously.

- The younger population who are comfortable to transact on online retailing.

Retailing in India

Indian grocers were perhaps among the first in the world to acquire professional retailing skills. There is the old story of a good retail grocer and the bad retail grocer in India.

Long ago, the **father of the nation, Mahatma Gandhi** realized the importance of the customer for the retailer; he is in fact the first to emphasize on the importance of customer relationship management practices in India. What he said about the importance of the customer is famous the world over. It goes like this:

"The customer is the most important person on our premises."

- ✓ He is not dependent on us, we are dependent on him.
- ✓ He is not an interruption of our work, he is the purpose of it.
- ✓ He is not an outsider on our business, he is part of it.
- ✓ We are not doing him a favour by serving him,
- ✓ He is doing us a favour by giving us the opportunity to do so."

A survey conducted by the Federation of Indian Chambers of Commerce and Industry (FICCI) and Price water house Coopers indicates that the Indian retail sector will undergo a sea change in size as well as format in the next 10 years. According to the survey, the established players will reach saturation levels in the metros by the year 2005 and shift their focus to other Class I cities.

Further it expects that by 2010 the country's top retailers will operate at least three to four formats, all scalable to size, location and providing value to their target customers. This diversity of formats will allow the company to make use of its brand value across different segments and categories of customers.

Global Overview of Retailing

With total sales of US$ 6.6 trillion, retailing is the world's largest private industry, ahead of finance and engineering. Some of the world's largest companies are in this sector: over 50 Fortune 500 companies are in this sector: over 50 fortunes 500 and around 25 of the Asian Top 200 firms are retailers. WalMart, the world's second largest retailer, has a turnover of US$ 260 billion, almost one third of India's GDP.

(Table 7: Top 10 retailers worldwide based on 2001 Annual Sales)

Rank	Retailers	Home Country	Sales
1	WalMart Stores, Inc.	USA	$202011
2	Carrefour Group	France	$62216
3	The Home Depot, Inc.	USA	$53553
4	The Kroger Co.	USA	$50098
5	Royal ahold	Netherlands	$48239

6	Metro AG	Germany	$43816
7	Target Corporation	USA	$39176
8	Albertson's Inc.	USA	$37931
9	Sears, Roebuck and Co.	USA	$37328
10	Kmart Corporation	USA	$36151
		Total Top 10	$612520

Source: Retail Forward, Inc.

Retailing in the developed world today is far more organized than in India. Up to 80% of all retail sales in the United States are accounted for by the organized retail sector. The corresponding figure in Western Europe is 70%, while it is 40% in Brazil and Argentina and 35% in Korea and Taiwan.

The Top Eighteen Retailers

According to the Deloitte 2006 Global Retailing Powers Study, US-based retailers represent 36 % of companies and 44.3% of their sales volume. Increased dollar-based sales and the international reach of European retailers have played a role in their relative increase versus the US-only strategy of many US retailers.

Top 18 Global retailers by retail sales in US$ million (Financial year 2004)

1. Walmart Stores Inc. (US): 285,222

2. Carrefour S.A. (FR): 89,568

3. The Home Depot Inc. (US): 73,094

4. Metro AG (DE): 69,781

5. Tesco plc (UK): 62,505

6. Kroger (US): 56,434

7. Costco Wholesale Corp. (US): 47,146

8. Target Corp. (US): 45,682

9. Koninklijke Ahlod N.v. (NL): 44,793

10. Schwarz Unternehmens Treuhand KG(DE): 42,793

11. Rewe-Zentral AG (DE): 42,782

12. ITM Development International/Intermarche (DE): 41,721

13. Albertsons (US): 39,897

14. Walgreen Co. (US): 37,508

15. Groupe Auchan S.A (FR): 37,373

16. AEON Co. Ltd. (JP): 36,345

17. Safeway, Inc. (US): 35,823

18. Sears, Roebuck & Co. (US): 35, 718

However, the boom in retailing has been confined primarily to the urban markets. There are two main reasons for this. Firstly, the modern retailer is yet to exhaust the opportunities in the urban market and has therefore probably not looked at other markets seriously. Secondly, the modern retailing trend, despite its cost effectiveness, has come to be identified with lifestyles. In order to appeal to all classes of the society, retail stores need to identify with different lifestyles. In a sense, this trend is already visible with the emergence of stores with an essentially value for money image. The attractiveness of the other stores actually appeals to the existing affluent class as well as those who aspire to be a part of it. Hence, one can assume that the retailing revolution is emerging along the lines of the economic evolution of society.

Growth of Malls in India

The Indian Government is taking major initiatives to aid growth in the retail sector. Investment in word class infrastructure is expected to be close to USD 150 bn.

- The hitherto restricted retail real estate sector was opened up for Foreign Direct Investment in 2005. As a result, Malls of international scale and quality are expected to come up;

- Mall growth is being seen as a clear indicator of the economic prosperity in India. Significantly, the number of Malls in the country has increased at a fast pace. And they are doing brisk business. A trip to the local Mall (there will be one in every locality soon!) will bear this out;

- From almost no Malls existing in the country over a decade ago, there were 96 operational Malls in August 2005.

- Here's more good news. This phenomenon is not restricted to major cities of the country alone. It has percolated to the "Tier II" and "Tier III" cities as well. The contribution of Tier II cities in organized retail sales is expected to be about 20-25%.

Number of Malls in Major Cities of India

Cities Name	2005	2007
Other Cities	34	86
Hyderabad	8	16
Bangalore	8	20
Pune	11	23
Kolkata	10	20
Chennai	2	6
Mumbai, Navi Mumbai, Thane	36	71
Noida and Ghaziabad	15	29
Gurgon	13	34
Delhi	21	51
Total	158	356

(Source: Crisil)

According to this year's Global Retail Development Index India is positioned as the leading destination for retail investment. This followed from the saturation in western retail markets and we find big western retailers like Walmart and Tesco entering in to India market.

India's retail industry accounts for 10% of its GDP and 8% of the employment to reach $17 billion by 2010. There are about 300 new Malls, 1,500 supermarkets and 325 departmental stores being built in the cities very soon.

Percentage

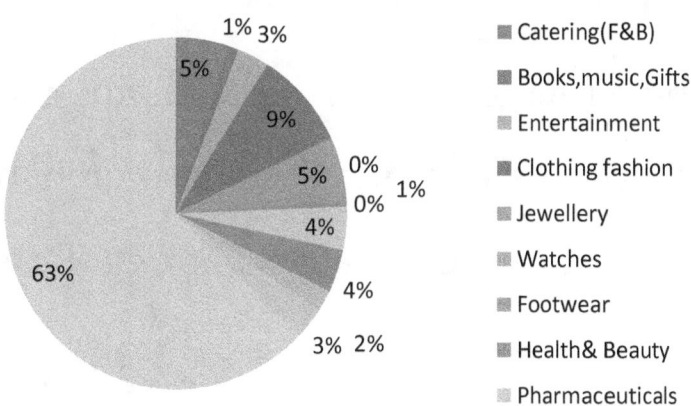

(The Indian Retail PIE 2006)

Percentage

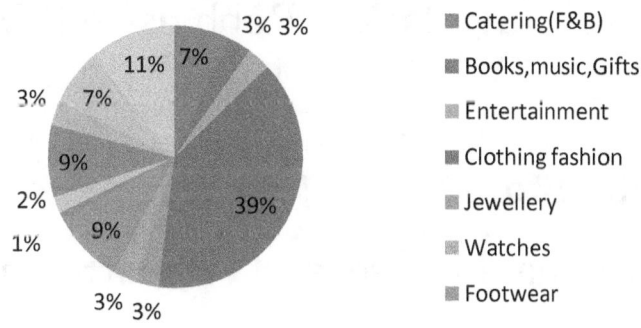

(The Organized Retail PIE 2006)

TYPES OF RETAILERS

Convenience store

Ideally located close to residential areas to enable target customers have easy accessibility and select convenient merchandise such as beverages, ready to eat snacks, grocery etc.

Chain of stores

A single retailer establishes a chain of stores with its exclusive store design, synergistic merchandising plan, promotion and service strategy. For eg. Raymond Chain of stores.

Franchise

Retail stores owned and operated by individuals on behalf of and licensed by a big supporting organization. For e.g. Pizza Hut, Baskin Robbins, NIIT, McDonalds etc.

Departmental Store

A store having several departments such as clothing, personal care and cosmetics, books and stationeries, house ware goods, electronic goods etc. all under single roof although individually functioning as a strategic business unit. These stores are large in size and area. For e.g. Big Bazaar.

Super Market

A store which is departmentalized with self service offering groceries, limited non food items such as health and beauty related items and general merchandise. Mini supermarkets with built up area of 1000 – 2000 sq.ft. and large ones 3500 – 5000 sq.ft. for e.g. food world outlets, nilgiris etc.

Hyper Market

Hyper markets are very large in size; carry grocery, hardware, appliances and other general merchandise, with self service facilities, usually located in warehouse type structures with large parking facilities. For e.g. Star India Bazaar, Giant of RPG Group and Big Bazaar.

Shopping Mall

A shopping Mall is the arrangement of retail stores and providing the right mix of shopping, food courts and entertainment and parking facilities. The retail space is shared by and anchor stores and other retailers who pays the developers of the Mall rent or lease payment for putting up the shop within the Mall premises.

Shopping Plaza

The shopping plazas are the configuration of many tenants using space of 1000 sq.ft. or so for putting up stores within a single building. For e.g. fountain plaza, Chennai, Modi Arcade Plaza, Bangalore.

Discount Stores

Discount store retail a broad variety of merchandize offer limited services at low prices. For e.g. Subiksha and Margin free supermarket.

Factory and seconds outlet

The factory stores are owned and operated by the manufacturers who sell discounted merchandise or factory seconds or cancelled orders to consumers at a low prices. For e.g. Bata factory outlet, Peter England Factory outlet etc.

KIOSK

KIOSK is a store often is concessions format store placed within a Mall / shopping center, a bus station, airport etc. It is a free standing pavilion open on one or more sides. For instance in a bookstore kiosk, customers are provided with online catalogue service to help them to identify titles and read reviews before making a purchase decision

ABOUT THE MALL

A Mall is the arrangement of retail stores and providing the right mix of shopping, food courts and entertainment and parking facilities.

The retail space is shared by anchor stores and other retailer who pays the developers of the Mall rent or lease payment for putting up the shop within the Mall premises. For e.g. pyramid Mall, Himalaya Mall etc.

Several Malls are coming up at Ahmedabad. New Malls are cropping up and existing ones are permitting the city with new branches. The Mall culture is catching up gradually in city with several Malls making their entry in Ahmedabad retail sector. These Malls have given a new dimension to shopping experience. Malls have transformed once compulsive and sober shopping in to a family entertainment and as a weekend pastime.

With the entire products available less than one complex, offering rich and pleasant ambience and stocking. Several big players of India and mega retailers of the world are choosing the city as their retail destination. During the last five years, the city had witnessed the development of Malls, hypermarkets, spread of supermarkets in every nook and corner of the city and emergence of several specialty stores. The factors for this rapid growth of retail industry in the city are the city boost of highest number of upper income households, spending habits of the citizens, relatively low real estate costs, and low risk of return ratio. The competition among retailers has become very stiff.

Retailers are widening their coverage area, crossing borders and shattering cultural barriers. Technological changes are playing a pivotal role in retail industry in providing better services and reduction in overhead costs.

Profile of Malls

Himalaya Mall

Himalaya Mall situated in the prime location of the city, Himalaya Mall is a centrally air conditioned Mall which has stores of all the major brands related to clothes men and women, shoes, accessories etc. Himalaya Mall located at near Indraprasth Tower, Drive in Road, Memnagar, Ahmedabad 380 052.

Pyramid Mall

Pyramid Mall is about one kilometer away from C.G.Road. It is a favorite destination amongst the locals of the city. It consists of many stores and ships of popular brand. It also has restaurants and coffee shop where you can enjoy during your shopping. Pyramid Mall located at near Parimal Garden, Elisbridge, Ahmedabad – 380 006.

Big Bazaar

Big Bazaar located in west Ahmedabad, Big Bazaar is one of the popular and famous Malls in the city. It comprises all the famous brands in categories of garments, electronics, cosmetics, accessories, shoes etc. under one roof. Big Bazaar located Nr. ISCON Temple, S.G. Highway, Ahmedabad.

Kshitij

The Mall is accessible from all parts of the city. With large residential developments coming up, it also has a strong consumer base. Given consumer preference and potential, the Mall has a lifestyle and fashion focus. Kshitij located at satellite road, Ahmedabad.

The Mall is complete shopping experience with the availability at choices, so many brands, impeccable ambience and food under one single roof.

Malls provide not only a great ambiance but shopping, entertainment and F&B options under one single roof.

Mall culture is catching on fast in India. It has become the way of shopping in metros and tier I cities. How this phenomenon is spreading fast in tier II cities as well. SMall tier III cities will also be gripped by this Mall culture in future.

Mall would provide suitable environment, particularly to the age group of 15 to 45 for shopping. Indian retail sector has undergone a complete transformation in recent times. For a long time, the corner grocery store was the only choice available to the consumer, especially in urban areas. From supermarkets and hypermarkets, to department stores and convenience stores and one stop shops, a retailing wave is currently sweeping the country.

The Mall culture is really gripping the Indian consumers because of more awareness, recent trends and changing lifestyles.

Indian retail boom is evident even in smaller towns and cities of the country where organized retail formats have increasingly become popular.Development of mega Malls in India is adding new dimensions to the booming retail sector.

No. of Malls in Ahmedabad

- ✓ Iscon Mall
- ✓ 10 Acres city Ma
- ✓ Croma
- ✓ Parsvanath
- ✓ Pyramid
- ✓ Alpha one
- ✓ Big Bazar
- ✓ Gallops
- ✓ Kshitij
- ✓ R3 the Mall
- ✓ Himalaya
- ✓ life Style
- ✓ R Cube

Chapter-5

Consumer Behavior towards Malls

(Consumer purchased products from the Mall)

Sr. No.	Purchase Products	Respondents	% of respondents
1	Yes	95	95
2	No	5	5
	Total	100	100

% of Respondents

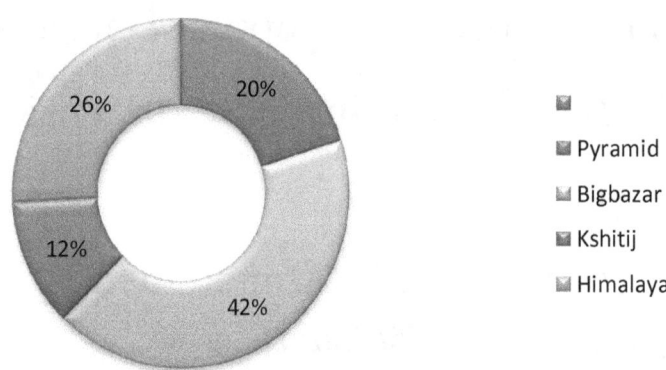

Pyramid
Bigbazar
Kshitij
Himalaya

(Visit the Malls monthly by consumers)

Sr. No.	Visit in a Month	Respondents	% of respondents
1	Once	20	20
2	Twice	26	26

3	Three	23	23
4	Fourth	10	10
5	Fifth	10	10
6	More	11	11

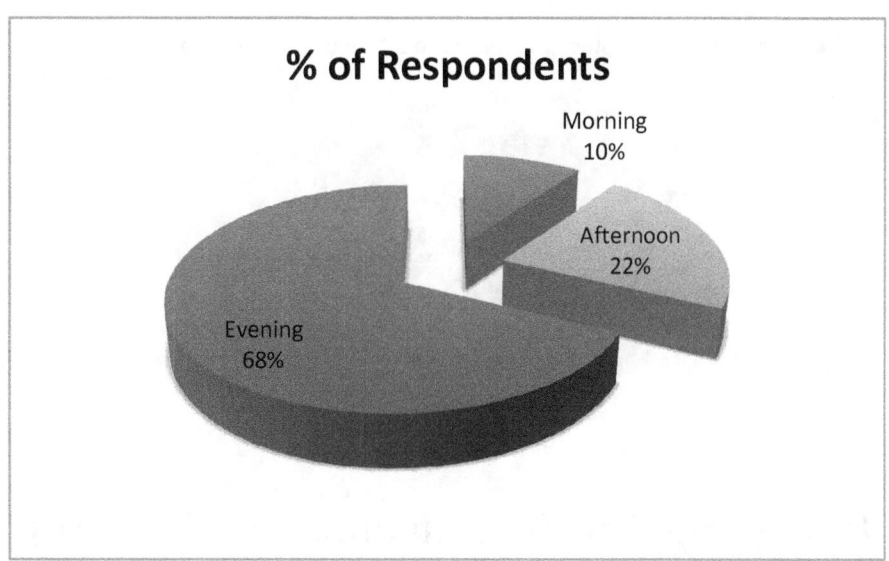

% of Respondents

Morning 10%

Afternoon 22%

Evening 68%

(Prefer Time for going in to the Mall)

(Consumers prefer day for going into the Mall.)

Sr. No.	Days	Respondents	% of respondents
1	Sunday	24	24
2	Monday	05	05
3	Tuesday	03	03
4	Wednesday	26	26

5	Thursday	09	09
6	Friday	01	01
7	Saturday	03	03
8	Any day	29	29

% of Respondents

▦ ▪ Less than 15 minutes ▪ 15 minute to 30 minute ▪ More than 30 minute

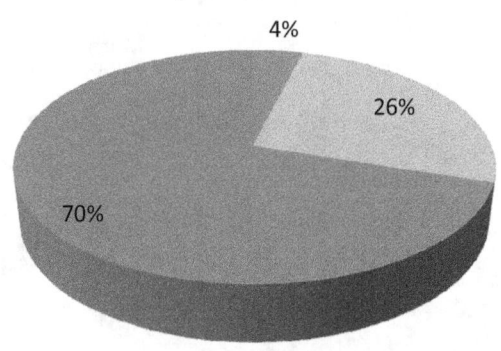

(Spending time by consumers in the Mall)

% of Respondents

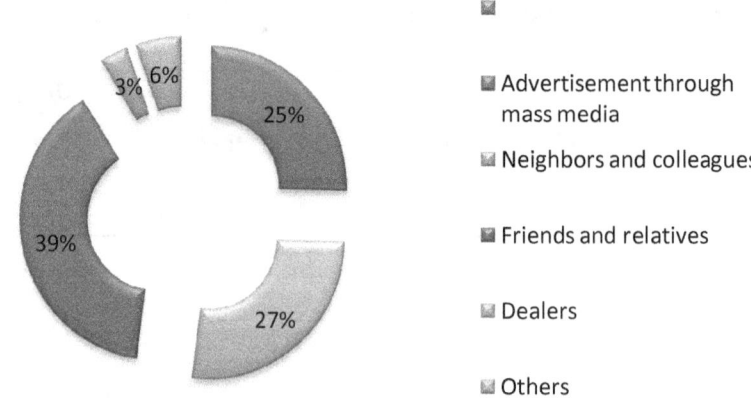

▪ Advertisement through mass media

▪ Neighbors and colleagues

▪ Friends and relatives

▪ Dealers

▪ Others

(Getting information by consumers about various Malls)

(Decision maker for the choice of Malls)

Sr. No.	Decision Maker	Respondents	% of respondents
1	Self	61	61
2	Spouse	17	17
3	Family member	39	39
4	Friends	31	31
5	Relatives	03	03
6	Others	03	03

(Preference of consumers towards facilities provide by Mall)

Sr. No	Facility	% of Respondents				
		Very Imp	Imp.	Neutral	Less Imp.	Not Imp.
1	Store atmosphere	58	26	15	01	00
2	Relaxation & enjoyment	27	41	26	06	00
3	More space	29	46	23	02	00

	to move in					
4	A good elevator system	24	42	26	08	00
5	Convenient layout at the Mall	26	34	25	10	05
6	Easily accessible billing canters	30	31	18	17	04
7	Trial rooms	43	28	19	05	05
8	Easily locatable stairs	36	38	19	03	04
9	Ample parking space	34	30	23	11	02
10	Prolonged experience	25	.44	18	11	02

| 11 | Promotion scheme | 37 | 27 | 21 | 11 | 04 |

(Consumer's opinion towards the service quality provided by different Mall)

Sr. No.	Mall	Service quality respondents (Percentage)			
		Fair	Good	Excellent	Poor
1	Pyramid	03	15	21	00
2	Big Bazaar	08	41	31	02
3	Kshitij	03	09	13	01
4	Himalaya	08	26	16	00

(Consumer's expenditure in a month towards purchasing product from Mall.)

Sr. No	Expenditure	Respondents	% of respondents
1	Less than 500	28	28
2	501 to 1000	42	42
3	1001 to 5000	25	25
4	5001 to 10000	04	04
5	More than	01	01

	10000		

(Problems face by consumers during choice of Malls)

Sr No.	Problems	Respondents	% of respondents
1	High price	38	38
2	Not a standardized product	19	19
3	Far from the home	44	44
4	Any other	23	23

(Customer satisfaction with sales service provided by Mall)

Sr No.	Customers Satisfaction	Respondents	% of respondents
1	High satisfied	24	24
2	Satisfied	68	68
3	Dissatisfied	07	07
4	Highly dissatisfied	01	01

% of Respondents

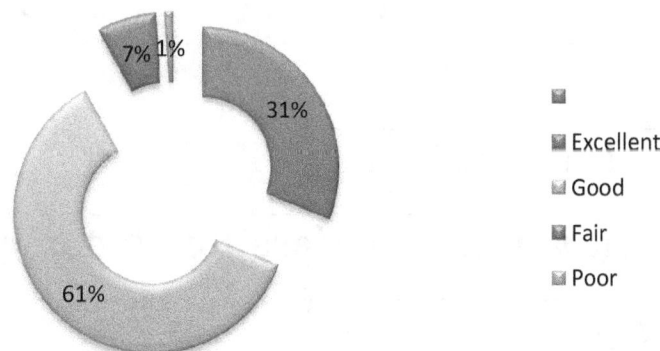

Legend:
- Excellent
- Good
- Fair
- Poor

7% 1% 31% 61%

(Consumers overall views towards Malls)

(Age wise classification of consumers)

Sr No.	Age	Respondents	% of respondents
1	Below 20	10	10
2	20 to 30	49	49
3	31 to 40	20	20
4	41 to 50	11	11
5	Above 50	10	10

(Gender wise classification of consumers)

Sr No.	Gender	Respondents	% of respondents
1	Male	59	59
2	Female	41	41

(Occupation wise classification of consumers)

Sr No.	Occupation	Respondents	% of respondents
1	Self employed	16	16
2	Services	18	18
3	Study	43	43
4	Professional	13	13
5	Any other	10	10

(Family income wise classification of consumer)

Sr No.	Family income	Respondents	% of respondents
1	Less than 2500	04	04
2	2501 to 5000	05	05

3	5001 to 10000	19	19
4	10001 to 15000	29	29
5	Above 15000	43	43

(Marital status wise classification of consumers)

Sr No.	Marital Status	Respondents	% of respondents
1	Married	46	46
2	Unmarried	54	54

HYPOTHESIS TESTING

Pyramid

(Facilities provided by Pyramid)

No.	Facility	Very Imp/ 5	Imp/ 4	Neutral /3	Less Imp/ 2	Not Imp/ 1	Total	Mean
1	Store Atmosph	85	20	9	0	0	114	4.56

	ere							
2	Relaxatio n and enjoymen t	35	36	24	2	0	97	3.88
3	More space to move in	45	48	12	0	0	105	4.20
4	A good elevator system	30	36	24	4	0	94	3.76
5	Convenie nt layout at the Malls	35	32	18	4	2	91	3.64
6	Easily accessible billing counters	40	28	9	12	1	90	3.60
7	Trail rooms	60	28	12	2	1	103	4.12
8	Easily locatable	40	40	15	2	1	98	3.92

	stairs							
9	Ample parking space	40	28	18	6	1	93	3.72
10	Prolonged experience	30	48	12	6	0	96	3.84
11	Promotion scheme	45	28	18	4	1	96	3.84
							Total	43.08
							Mean	3.92

Big Bazaar

(Facilities provided by Big Bazaar)

No.	Facility	Very Imp/5	Imp/4	Neutral/3	Less Imp/2	Not Imp/1	Total	Mean
1	Store Atmosphere	65	28	12	2	0	107	4.28

2	Relaxation and enjoyment	30	48	15	4	0	97	3.88
3	More space to move in	35	48	18	0	0	101	4.04
4	A good elevator system	35	32	21	6	0	94	3.76
5	Convenient layout at the Malls	35	28	21	6	1	91	3.64
6	Easily accessible billing counters	50	20	15	8	1	94	3.76
7	Trail rooms	55	24	15	2	2	98	3.92
8	Easily locatable stairs	50	36	12	2	1	101	4.04
9	Ample parking space	45	36	15	4	0	100	4.00
10	Prolonged	35	32	18	6	1	92	3.68

	experience						
11	Promotion scheme	50	24	18	4	1	97	3.88
						Total	**42.88**
						Mean	**3.90**

Kshitij

(Facilities provided by Kshitij)

No.	Facility	Very Imp/5	Imp/4	Neutral/3	Less Imp/2	Not Imp/1	Total	Mean
1	Store Atmosphere	75	24	12	0	0	111	4.44
2	Relaxation and enjoyment	40	36	18	4	0	98	3.92
3	More space to move in	25	56	15	2	0	98	3.92
4	A good elevator system	20	60	15	2	0	97	3.88
5	Convenient	20	36	27	4	1	88	3.52

	layout at the Malls							
6	Easily accessible billing counters	25	52	12	4	1	94	3.76
7	Trail rooms	65	24	12	2	1	104	4.16
8	Easily locatable stairs	45	36	18	0	1	100	4.00
9	Ample parking space	40	24	21	6	1	92	3.68
10	Prolonged experience	25	52	9	6	1	93	3.72
11	Promotion scheme	50	24	15	6	1	96	3.84
							Total	42.84
							Mean	3.89

Himalaya

(Facilities provided by Himalaya)

No.	Facility	Very Imp/5	Imp/4	Neutral/3	Less Imp/2	Not Imp/1	Total	Mean
1	Store Atmosphere	65	32	12	0	0	109	4.36
2	Relaxation and enjoyment	30	44	21	2	0	97	3.88
3	More space to move in	40	32	24	2	0	98	3.92
4	A god elevator system	35	40	18	4	0	97	3.88
5	Convenient layout at the Malls	40	40	9	6	1	96	3.84
6	Easily accessible billing counters	35	24	18	10	1	88	3.52
7	Trail rooms	35	36	18	4	1	94	3.76
8	Easily locatable stairs	45	40	12	2	1	100	4.00

9	Ample parking space	45	32	15	6	0	98	3.92
10	Prolonged experience	35	44	15	4	0	98	3.92
11	Promotion scheme	40	32	12	8	1	93	3.72
							Total	42.72
							Mean	3.88

(Satisfaction level of consumers)

Satisfaction level Malls	Highly satisfied /5	Satisfied /4	Dissatisfied /3	Highly satisfied /2	Not at all satisfied /1	Total	Mean
Pyramid	35	64	6			105	4.20
Big Bazaar	30	68	3	2		103	4.12
Kshitij	25	72	6			103	4.12
Himalaya	30	68	6			104	4.16
	Total						16.6
	Mean						4.15

(Overall behavior of consumers towards Malls)

No.	Malls	Mean
1.	Pyramid	3.92
2.	Big Bazaar	3.90
3.	Kshitij	3.89
4.	Himalaya	3.88
	Total	15.59
	Mean	3.90

It is evident from above table that various facilities provide by Malls to consumers during study period (according to selected respondents). It shows overall grade 3.90, i.e. nearly important.

From above table it can be say that, the overall satisfaction level of consumers are 4.15, i.e. nearly satisfied. Whereas the facilities level provided by various Malls to consumers are 3.90, i.e. nearly important. It means consumers are satisfied with facilities provided by various Malls.

So, from above result we can reject the null hypothesis and we can accept the alternative hypothesis.

Chapter-6

Findings and Suggestions

FINDINGS

While discussing with 100 (hundred) consumers and management of 4 (four) Malls. Consumers were interviewed and requested to answer the questionnaire. They were contacted personally to avoid misunderstanding. On the basis of data analysis and interpretation many findings were found, the findings are as follows:

- There are so many Malls in Ahmedabad but most of consumers visited Big Bazaar.

- Majority of consumers preferred purchase products form Malls.

- Most of consumers visited the Malls twice in a month.

- Consumers prefer evening time for the Malls.

- Most of consumers select any day or Wednesday for going in to the Malls.

- Majority of consumers spend more than 30 minutes in the Malls.

- It was observed that most of consumers get information through their friends and relatives.

- It was found that most of consumers take decision for the choice of Malls by themselves.

- Majority of consumers favoured store atmosphere facility, trail rooms and ample parking space and promotion schemes are very important.

- There are many facilities provided by Malls to consumers but customer preferred relaxation and enjoyment, more space to move in a good elevator system, convenient layout at the Malls, easily accessible billing counters and easily locatable stairs, prolonged experience important for consumer.

- Most of consumers purchase regulatory clothes, food and cosmetics from Malls.

- Majority of consumers prefer grocery, books, entertainment, electronics items, furniture and home décor sometimes.

- Consumer opinion towards sales services provided by Pyramid is very excellent.

- It is evident that most of consumers spend money ranging from Rs. 501/- to Rs. 1000/- for purchasing a product from Mall.

- Majority of surveyed respondents reported that so far they have had far from the home during choice of Malls.

- Most of respondents reported that they are satisfied with the sales services provided by Malls.

- The study found that the respondents overall experience of the Malls are good.

- The age group in between 21-30 years accounts for the highest (49%) of the sample respondents.

- The study reveals the majority (59%) of the respondents have fallen in the male group.

- Majority of the respondents are studying

- Most of respondent's family earning monthly income of Rs. 15000 and above.

- Most of consumers are unmarried.

- Most of Malls are interested in providing better services to customers.

- Malls management is interested in providing store atmosphere, a good elevator system, easily accessible billing counters, trial rooms easily locatable stairs, ample parking space are very important for Malls.

- There are many facilities are also important for Malls such as convenient lay out at the Mall, prolonged experience, promotion schemes, relaxation and enjoyment, more space to move in all are also important for Malls.

- Malls are supplied most of information to consumers about offers through newspapers, hoardings and their armachment systems.

- According to Malls the most of consumers prefer evening time for visit the Mall.

- Most of consumers prefer Sunday, Wednesday and any day for visit the Mall.

- It was found that most of consumers spend more than 30 minutes in the Mall.

- It was observed that food demand regularly and electronics and home décor demand sometimes in the Malls by consumers.

- Malls are thinking towards providing better services to consumer help to improve the retail market.

- Most of consumers say that store atmosphere facility is very important in all Malls.

- Majority of consumers say that easily accessible billing counter was neutral in Pyramid and Himalaya Mall.

- Most of consumer say that convenient layout at Mall was neutral in Big Bazaar and Kshitij Mall.

SUGGESTIONS

- Pyramid and Kshtij should advertise their services towards consumers through advertising of mass media or other sources. So that they increase the rush of consumers towards their Mall.

- There should be continuous research and development for the development of the Mall.

- Retailers should keep themselves and the units updated with the latest extrant product in the market to retain their consumers.

- Mass media like television, newspapers etc. are to be extensively used for the purpose of publicity.

- The customer has to keep himself always updated with the latest development in the retail industry so that he can reap the maximum benefits offered by the retailers.

- Consumers can restrict their purchases within their budget for provisions.

- Now a day's various services provided by retailer, the customer can derive the maximum benefits and comforts from his purchase.

- The customer may check the authenticity in schemes and may calculate real benefit.

- Pyramid and Himalaya Mall should increase easily accessible billing counters for consumers.

- Big Bazaar and Kshitij Mall should improve the convenient layout in the Mall.

References

- **Books**

  - Bansal S.P, Verma O.P., Marketing Research, Ludhiana, Kalyani Publishers, First Edition, 2007.

  - Berman Barry and Evans, R. Joel, Retail Management: A Strategic Approach, New Delhi, Pearson Eduction Asia, Eight Edition, 2002.

  - Bose Biplab S., Marketing Management [Taxes & Cases] Mumbai, Himalaya Publishing, House, First Edition, 2007.

  - Chunawalla S.A, Commentary on Consumer Behavior, Mumbai, Himalaya Publishing House, Millennium, Reprint Edition, 2001.

  - Chunawalla S.A., Contours of Retailing Management, Mumbai, Himalaya Publishing House, First Edition, 2006.

  - Chunawalla S.A., Marketing Principles and Practices, Mumbai, Himalaya Publishing House, Second Edition, 2006.

- Dhotre, Meenal, Channel Management and Retail Marketing, Mumbai, Himalaya Publishing House, First Edition, 2005.

- Kothari C.R., Research Methodology Methods and Techniques, New Delhi, Wishwa Prakashan, Second Edition.

- Kotler Philip, Marketing Management, Delhi, Pearson educationPte. Ltd., Eleventh Edition, 2003.

- Levy, Michad and Weitz A barton, Retailing Management, New Delhi, Tata McGraw-Hill Publishing Co. Ltd., Fifth Edition, 2003.

- Malhotra Naresh K., Marketing Research- An applied Orientation, New Delhi, Prentice-Hall of India Pvt. Ltd., Fourth Edition, 2005.

- Nair Suja R., Consumer Behavior and Marketing Research, Mumbai, Himalaya Publishing House, Forth Edition, 2007.

- Nair Suja, Retail Management, Mumbai, Himalaya Publishing House, First Edition, 2006.

- Ramaswamy V.S., Namakumari S., Marketing Management, New Delhi, McMillan India Pvt. Ltd., Third Edition, 2002.

- Schiffman Leon G. and Kanuk Leslie Lazar, Consumer Behavior, New Delhi, Prentice-Hall of India Pvt. Ltd., Sixth Edition, 2001.

- Sherlekar S.A., Marketing Management, Mumbai, Himalaya Publishing House, Reprint-2002.

- Sonatakki C.N., Principle of Marketing, Ludhiana, Kalyani Publishers, First Edition, 2000.

- Sontakki C.N., Marketing Management, Mumbai, Himalaya Publishing House, First Edition, 2006.

- Vedmani Gibson G., Retail Management functional Principles & Practices, Mumbai, Jaico Publishing House, Second Edition, Revised & Enlarged, 2004.

- **Magazines and Journals**

- 4PS Business and Marketing, Vol.-2, issue 11, 6 July-19 July, 2007.

- Business India, November 18, 2007.

- Business Today, Fortnightly Magazine, December 16, 2007.

- Indian Journal of Marketing, Volume -37, No. 10, October-2007.

- Indian Journal of Marketing, Volume -37, No. 11, November-2007.

- Indian Journal of Marketing, Volume -37, No. 3, March-2005.

- Indian Journal of Marketing, Volume -37, No. 3, March-2007.

- Indian Journal of Marketing, Volume -37, No. 4, April-2006.

- Indian Journal of Marketing, Volume -37, No. 8, August-2007.

- Indian Management Vol.-44, issue 6, June 2005.

- Retail Vol. 7, No.1, January, 2008.

- Retail, Vol.-6, No.9, September, 2007.

- Retailer, India Edition, Vol. -2, No. 4, 15th August – 30th September, 2007.

- Retailer, India Edition, Vol. -2, No. 5, October, 2007.

- Retailer, India Edition, Vol. -2, No. 8, 15th January- 14th February, 2008.

- Synergy-I.T.S Journal of I.T. & Management, Volume-5, No. 2, July-2007.

- Synergy-I.T.S Journal of I.T.% & Management, Volume-5, No. 2, July-2007.

- The ICFAI Journal of Management Research, Vol.-6, No.6, 2007.

Newspapers

- The Economic Times, Sunday, 30th December, 2007.

- The Economic Times, Monday, 31st December, 2007.

- The Economic Times, Thursday, 14th February, 2008.

- **Webliography**

  - www.ahmedabadline.com
  - www.economictimes.com
  - www.enwikipedia.org
  - www.google.com
  - www.gujaratglobal.com
  - www.imagesretail.com
  - www.indiacatalog.com
  - www.indianbusiness.nic.in
  - www.indiaretailing.com
  - www.justdial.com
  - www.ksatechnopak.com
  - www.mouthshut.com
  - www.retailindustry.com
  - www.retailnews.com
  - www.retailsector.co.in
  - www.timesofindia.indiatimes.com
  - www.walmart.com
  - www.yahoo.com

www.ingramcontent.com/pod-product-compliance
Lightning Source LLC
Chambersburg PA
CBHW080600180526
45168CB00007B/2723